this dog notebook belongs to:

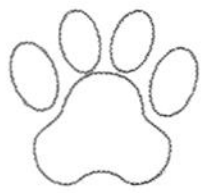

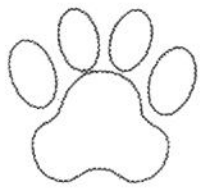

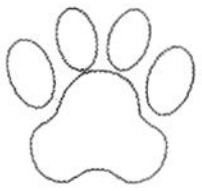

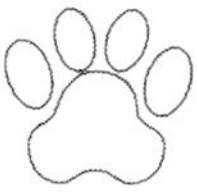

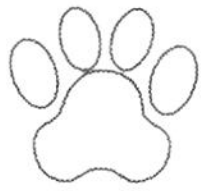

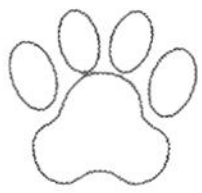

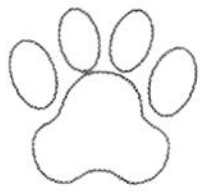

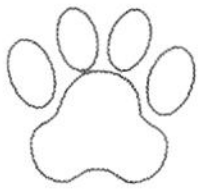

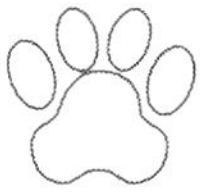

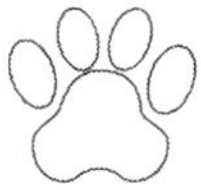

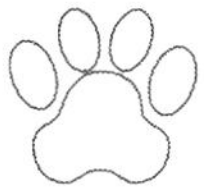

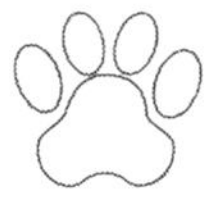

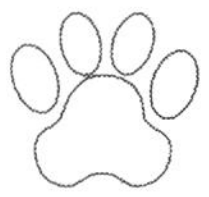

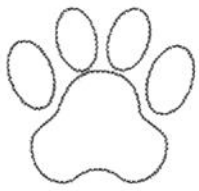

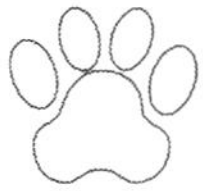

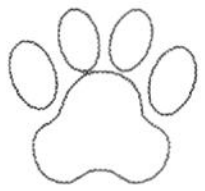

Made in the USA
Las Vegas, NV
29 October 2021

33327732R00061